Make Money Online Entrepreneur Series:

Book 9
List Building
with
Twitter

KIP PIPER
http://www.kippiperbooks.com

YOUR FREE GIFT…

Want a free book? Want access to more freebies and special offers through Amazon?

As a way of saying *thanks* for your purchase, I'm offering a free eBook that is only available to my customers. Right now, you can get a copy of my book: *"28-Day Small Business Profit Plan: The Quick Start Guide for Business Success"*. This book is not sold anywhere else and can only be found on my website.

Plus, you will learn how to get instant notification whenever there is a new free book or special book bundles through Amazon.

Get the details at my website: **www.KipPiperBooks.com**

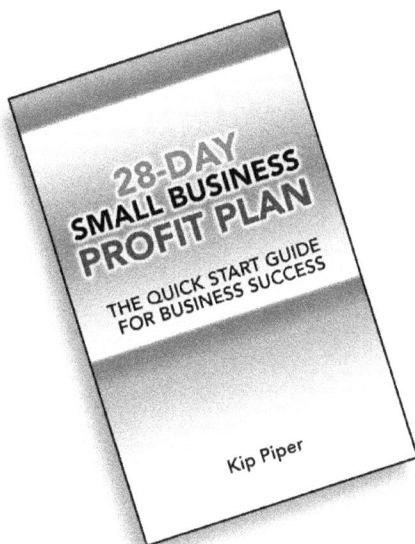

CONTENTS

AUTHOR'S NOTE

As you have probably experienced, the Internet and the websites on it are constantly changing. The information, examples, and screenshots presented in this book are accurate at the time of publication.

If you encounter any websites that have changed, please let me know by emailing me at: **kip@kippiperbooks.com**.

Remember, even though the website(s) may have changed, the principles, techniques and strategies in this book remain sound.

The links in this book are primarily affiliate links, which means if you purchase through the links, the price is the same to you and I receive a commission. This is the heart of affiliate marketing and entrepreneurship – which I am teaching you how to do with this book! I thank you in advance for using the affiliate links.

A FEW WORDS FROM KIP

Before I began teaching others how to blog and be successful with their online businesses, I wanted to be sure that I had something different to teach – strategies that are not easily found but can make a huge impact on success. The last thing I wanted to do is waste anyone's time. I wanted to offer something unique that would add both value and the potential for quick success for you.

Unknowingly, my research into online business success began in 1996 when I was first introduced to the concept of affiliate marketing. The potential for income excited me and I was quick to start experimenting with it. I joined Amazon.com and the few other affiliate programs available at the time. I added links on my website to products that related to my web design and Internet marketing business, with the purpose of offering quality resources to my website visitors and my clients. I encouraged and worked with my clients to include affiliate marketing in their overall online presence. I did this all in the hopes of adding to my income streams and eventually have affiliate marketing my dominant, if not sole, source of income.

But it did not come quickly, as others had promised or experienced. I totally, 100% believed in the concept of an online business and affiliate marketing (and still do), I understood the mechanics of setting up websites, creating products, and adding affiliate links, but I struggled with ranking my site high with the search engines and driving traffic to my site. Where were all the promised visitors who would buy what I offered or recommended so I could earn commissions?

Why were so many others achieving success? Why wasn't I experiencing the same success? Where was I going wrong?

I joined various mastermind groups. I purchased training programs from so-called "gurus". I bought books, read articles, watched videos, attended conference calls and webinars – I immersed myself in learning about blogging, affiliate marketing, and creating products.

The one most important thing I learned is that you need multiple websites, each focused on a different niche, to ensure a steady stream of income. "But," I asked, "if I can't get people to come to my first website, why should I spend more money and time creating websites that will not be visited either?" And each "guru" smiled nicely and said, "If you will upgrade your membership to our most expensive level, I'll tell you." But when I looked closely, I realized each "guru" was not living the life I wanted. In fact, most were working as hard or harder than I – with even less free time and income! They did not have the freedom of time and money that I wanted.

I didn't give up, though. I continued my search – knowing the one little "missing link" was out there.

One day I found it!

With this new knowledge, I knew without a doubt I could not only be personally successful with blogging, affiliate marketing and product creation, but now I could teach others those same strategies.

I realized that knowledge is what sets apart the training I offer – with this book and my other books which you can find at **http://www.kippiperbooks.com**.

This book is unique because it was written for *YOU*.

- YOU are someone who sees the potential in having an online business of affiliate marketing and product creation, but needs to know how to get started.
- YOU want practical strategies and advice that have already been tested and proven to work.
- YOU are ready for double-digit growth in sales.
- YOU are committed to following through with what you're about to learn.

This is why YOU are here.

Now please understand. Every piece of advice, strategy and practice has been tested on actual live blog, affiliate marketing and product websites – my own, my clients', and others. None of this is theory. You might then ask yourself, *ok, so how many blogs and affiliate websites has Kip done and what qualifies her as an "internet business expert"?* I think that's a great question. I wish more people questioned so called "experts" to see what qualifies them. As for me, I looked back on the last 15 years of stats and discovered that I have personally generated a 5-figure income in blogging, affiliate marketing and my own product sales – and that's just part-time!

If that's something you'd like to accomplish, you've selected the right book and series to begin with. I say "begin" because you'll soon discover that the learning process is a journey.

But don't worry! There's one more thing that qualifies me to lead you down this path – I'm just like you. It doesn't matter if you've never built a website or if you're already earning an income with blogging, affiliate marketing and your own product, and simply want to improve your sales. As you have already read, I've been wherever you are right now.

For anyone who reads this book and the entire *"Make Money Online Entrepreneur Series"*, and implements everything they learn, I can guarantee your business will move forward with more subscribers, sales and a stronger connection to your market. Like I said before, it doesn't matter if you've never built a website in your life or if you're already experienced, I've been there and can show you how to make blogging, affiliate marketing and product creation a successful income source.

But before we begin, I need you to do something. Connect with me on Facebook at:

http://www.facebook.com/TheRandomBlondeFanPage

I'd love to stay in touch and learn more about your journey.

You also are invited to check my website for more business books, and all of the books included in this *"Making Money Online Entrepreneur Series"*:

http://www.kippiperbooks.com

Thanks again for choosing to spend this time with me. Now let's get started!

"Done is better than Perfect!"

INTRODUCTION

This is Book 9 of the *"Make Money Online Entrepreneur Series"*: *"List Building with Twitter"*.

The entire series consists of more than 20 books, specifically written as an entire online business success training course.

Beginning in August 2013, I released one book a week, in the proper order to ensure success. If you follow the series from Book 1 to the end, one week per book, you will complete a 5+ month training course and master being an online entrepreneur! Of course, you can finish the series faster. Just make sure you fully complete the lessons in each book before moving on to the next. This way your success will be greater!

This series is carefully designed to give you every building block you need to build a successful online business. All of the guesswork is taken away, and by following this series, you will avoid most of the common mistakes made by new and even experienced online entrepreneurs. All is revealed – nothing is left out!

The beauty of this series is that you can pick up any book on whatever topic you need at this moment. Or you can purchase each book as it is released. Or ultimately, you can purchase the entire series in a bundle!

However you choose to use the information offered in this and the other books, you will be moving forward with intention and strategy for success in your business.

If at any time you have questions or desire personal one-on-one coaching for a particular topic, feel free to contact me at **kip@kippiperbooks.com**.

Here's to your online business success!

ONLINE BUSINESS SUCCESS CORE VALUES

Before we get started, it is important to understand, to be a successful online business entrepreneur, it is necessary that you stay focused on your business and have the core values that ensure that success. Here are the values that I have found to be essential to keeping focused and moving forward. These values will be at the beginning of every book of this *"Make Money Online Entrepreneur Series"*.

Be Passionate About Entrepreneurship

As it says, you need to be passionate about what you do and about being an entrepreneur. Being an entrepreneur will present the greatest challenges and the greatest joy you've ever experienced in the business world.

Commit 100% And GO FOR IT

One of the biggest things about being successful is being okay with putting yourself out there. Even if it's just a part-time business, commit 100% of yourself to the time you invest in your business. Commit to see it through and don't give up too soon. As the saying goes, "Don't give up before the miracle happens." Be patient and be persistent.

Build A Network of Support & influence

You must build a network of support and influence. This means building your Facebook community, building your Twitter community, and building your LinkedIn community. You must contribute to other people and help them be successful. By contributing to others and helping them be successful, you will become successful.

Get Comfortable with Being Uncomfortable

You're going to be doing a lot of things that you may or may not have done in the past. You can only grow when you're uncomfortable. When you're feeling comfortable and used to doing the things that you normally do, it's really difficult to grow, so you need to be comfortable with being uncomfortable see you can stretch and grow.

Consistent Growth & Improvement

It is important that you commit to consistent growth and improvement. We all need improvement especially if we are to grow and become successful, because staying up to date with the current tools and resources is essential. What helps you with consistent growth and continuing to improve is tracking your progress on irregular basis.

You also need to be okay with evaluating yourself and looking back at what you did and what you didn't do – without judgment. Simply observe and then recommit to the next step of growth and improvement.

80/20 Rule & Speed of Implementation

I'm sure you would've heard of the 80/20 rule (also known as Pareto's Rule) that 20% of what you do provides 80% of your success. So you need to understand that not everything you do is going to be perfect. Learn from it and move on. The quicker you get things done with the knowledge that you have, the more you'll be able to grow.

Flexible Persistence

Be persistent with everything that you do, and stay consistent with everything you do. The ones who experience the most success are the ones who are persistent in accomplishing their goals and are the most consistent in what they do. To be consistent, you must commit to regularly completing the tasks that ensure your success, whether those tasks occur daily, weekly, monthly, etc.

Surround Yourself With "A" Players

In business you deserve to surround yourself with the best and those who share your entrepreneurial spirit. You become like those you spend your time with. So choose carefully who you hang around with, so you are with those who think like you and make you stretch and reach higher.

The same goes for your employees. If you're going to outsource, you must select the best people who are competent and people you will enjoy working with. Avoid people who have negative attitudes. Surround yourself with those who embrace the concepts of small business success, entrepreneurship, and financial wealth.

Sell With Conviction

Be passionate about your product or service. Make sure you understand every aspect of it so that you can easily describe its features and benefits to your potential customers. If you have hesitations or doubts about your product, improve it so you don't have doubts.

Celebrate All Wins

Celebrate all victories! When you get that first sale, celebrate that first sale. Celebrate each new client. Celebrate each year of business success. Make sure you celebrate all wins. This is really important to maintain passion, momentum and to ensure success.

INTRODUCTION TO TWITTER

In this book we are discussing all things Twitter. Twitter can be a great place to build a following and get your information out there, such as your free content. It's also a great way to build a list, and you can build a list very quickly by using Twitter.

What's really important about Twitter is that you want to be consistent. In this book are chapters about how you can use Twitter, how you can leverage it, just simply held understand it! If you've never used Twitter before, there's some terminology that you will need to learn and understand. We will go through all of these and more in this book.

In this introduction, what you need to understand is that Twitter is a great way for you to build a general list. But Twitter is not a great place to sell your product or service.

If you purchased and have read *Book 8 – List Building with Facebook* **http://www.kippiperbooks.com/book8** of this series, Twitter is very similar. It's a platform with over 240 million users that you can gain access to and have a presence with. But it's not a great place to sell directly.

What do I mean by this? When you go through the chapters in this book and set up your account, you're going to understand that you can share links on Twitter. Sharing links directly to your sales page, or to somebody else's sales page if you're promoting an affiliate offer, is not always the most effective strategy.

In talking about Twitter, it's preferable to take your followers, build a list and get them into your existing email and sales funnels.

So what do you promote on Twitter? Send your Twitter followers to a squeeze page perhaps where you give away a free offer. Send them to a free webinar registration. Send them to a blog post, which means any time you write a blog, you want to use Twitter to help you promote that blog post and drive traffic to your site. What's going to happen when they go to your blog? You're going to have an opt-in form where they can opt in and download, for example, a free guide or whatever is your free often offer.

That's the purpose of Twitter. It's a huge list with which you want to communicate on a regular basis. This is really important. It's important when you're on Twitter that there is a consistent level of communication.

It doesn't matter if it's every day, every 3 days, or every week. Consistency is what is important. So however often you have decided to communicate with your Twitter followers – whether it's once a day or once a week, etc. – you should remain consistent with the level and amount that you tweet.

One way that is very easy to do this – to get one tweet posted per week – if you or your Virtual Assistant (VA) is writing a blog post once a week, tweet the blog post.

Inspirational quotes are also great items to tweet and share on Twitter.

Remember, the purpose of Twitter is not just to attract followers. You hear people say, "I have 20,000 followers!" It's not the number of followers you have – you want to get those followers over to your free content, and more importantly, get them to join your email list. You want them to opt in – whether it's a squeeze page with a free offer, whether it's registering for a free webinar, whether it's to a blog post where they have the opportunity to opt in, etc.

Just like with Facebook, it's taking this free list of people on Twitter with whom you're communicating and converting them to your email list.

So as you go through this book, understand the basics of Twitter, understand how to leverage Twitter, understand the terminology, but keep in mind your building your Twitter list so you can convert them to your email list and then sell your products and your affiliate products to them in the future.

In this book, we are going to cover:

- The Mindset for Twitter
- Optimizing Your Profile for Success
- What You Should be Saying for Success on Twitter
- Mistakes to Avoid
- How to Avoid Getting Band
- Fast Track to Followers
- Tools for Twitter

Twitter is regularly changing their interface. The examples in this book are based on Twitter at the time of writing. While the Twitter interface may have changed when you read this book, the principles are the same. The information I'm providing in this book was accurate at the time of writing.

UNDERSTANDING TWITTER

It is pretty well understood that you don't get on Twitter and talk about what you ate for breakfast, what you had for lunch, or that you're getting coffee, or that you're doing this or that you're doing that. You can post those kinds of updates, but in general, Twitter is best used as an engaging and listening tool for your audience.

You want to put comments out there that engage your audience, that get them to respond back and then respond back to their responses. This is the easiest and fastest way to build a good audience and a loyal group of people that follow you and read your tweets.

So this is a mindset you want to have. You don't want to have the majority of your tweets about how you just got up, eating breakfast, etc.

Now you can put out personal tweets from time to time, especially if it's something funny about whatever you're doing. But in general, you want to post tweets that inspire people to respond back and engage with you.

A lot of people think that Twitter is a great tool for selling things and broadcasting a message to their audience. While that's true, I have found that some of the best uses are to build your audience, interact with them, engage with them, and then drive them to the blog or website with articles, and from there capture them into your email list.

I see a lot of people get on Twitter and just put out constant updates – they don't interact with anybody else, they don't respond to people, and they pretty much get zero results out of their efforts. The matter how big or small your following, Twitter is a social environment, so you really want to be social with your followers. This can be accomplished in just a few minutes a day if you approach it correctly.

How Twitter works is pretty simple. Here is a quick overview, assuming that you know most of this already. If not, you'll learn a couple of things with this overview.

Below is a screenshot of my Twitter page.

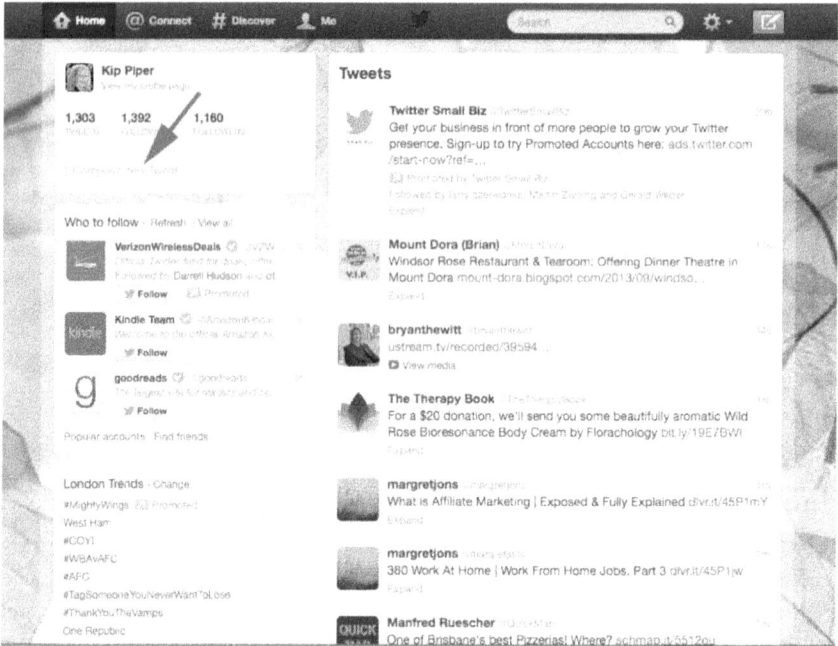

As indicated by the red arrow above, you click on the field "Compose new Tweet…" and it opens to a larger field – as you can see in the next screen shot below.

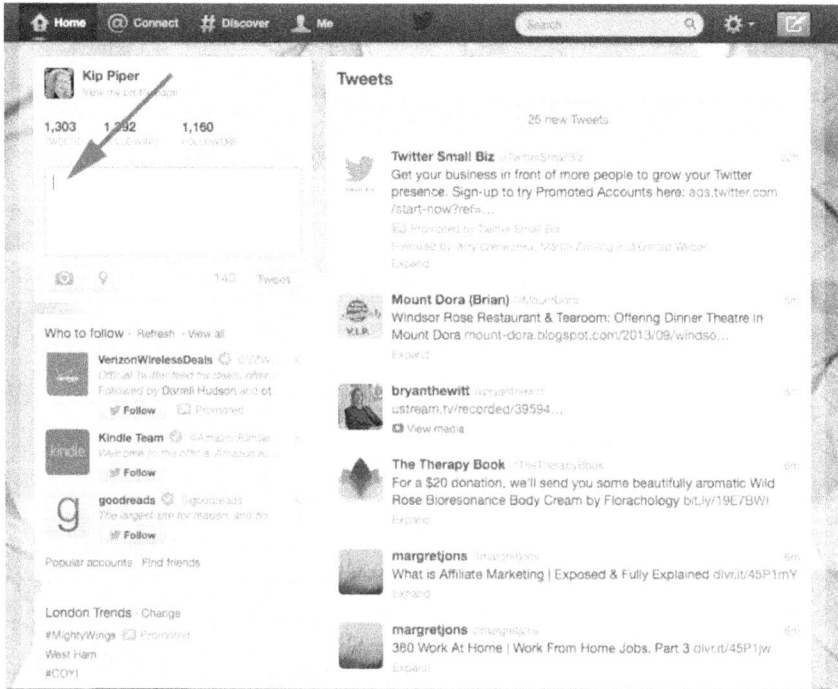

You type a message into this larger field – whatever you want your message to be – hit the "Tweet" button and your message to all of your followers. Your followers will see your tweets on their home screen, or if they have set up lists, they will see your message there (which we will cover in this book).

It's that simple!

When To Say What

You need to keep in mind that there are some key times you want to consider when posting information on your Twitter feed. Another words, it's been said that, at any given time, only 10% of your audience is online. This is really good information to know. For example, if you send a message out at 8 AM, you could probably send the same message back out at noon and get equal results.

So if you want to drive traffic to your blog, you can send information out at multiple times during the day.

Now there are certain times of day that the Twitter traffic is heavier then at others, you can see from the screenshot below.

Twitter Activity By Time of Day

The Facts: During the day, the most Twitter activity happens from 11 a.m. to 3 p.m. (EST)

Tweet Activity by Hour of the Day

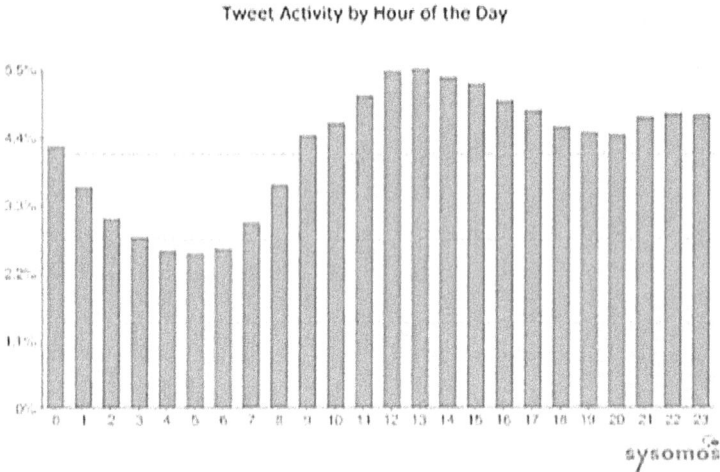

sysomos

Typically, this would depend on your audience and wear your audience is located. For me, being in the United States, the majority of my audience is on the East Coast, so the East Coast time frame works pretty well.

The type of information you put out, based on your audience and when they are reading it, is important as well. What I mean by that is, I found that in the morning inspiring and educational types of tweets are well received and get a lot of retweets and a lot of engagement. But funny or comedy posts don't seem to do as well in the morning or early afternoon, but the late afternoon and evening funny posts get great traction. On the flipside, if I put out a motivational quote or something inspiring in the late afternoon or evening, it's rare that I'll get much interaction.

I find that people want to be inspired or motivated in the mornings, and in the evenings they want to be entertained. They get on Twitter at those times of the day particularly for those purposes. So keep this in mind with your audience and when you are marketing to them.

Here are a few more basics about Twitter:

"@" Symbol

When someone posts a message with an "@" symbol in front of the username, as seen in the screenshot below, that's a way of addressing somebody.

If somebody wanted to send a tweet to me, they would just type in the "@" symbol and then my username "kip_piper" like this: @kip_piper. That message then would go directly to me via what is called the "@Connect" section. The "@Connect" section is on everybody's Twitter screen and you can find it at the top of your Twitter screen as indicated by the red arrow in the screenshot below.

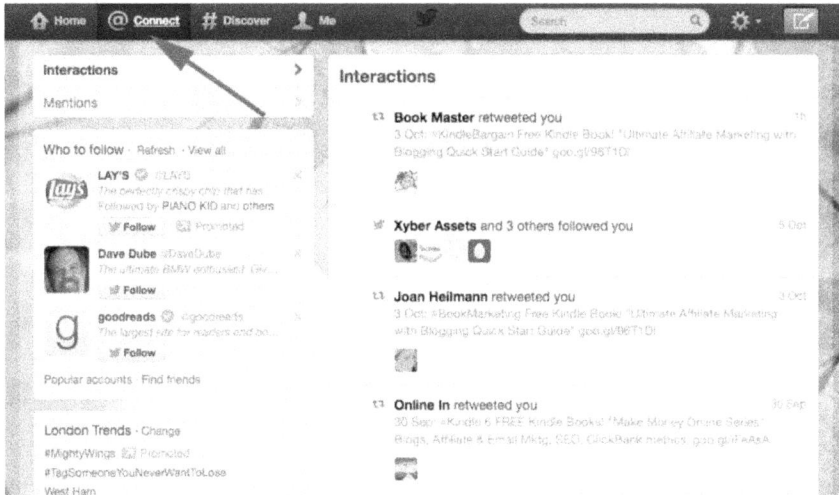

When you click on "@Connect", you will see all of the tweets for people who have included your information within their tweets.

Remember, when you start your tweet with the "@" symbol, the tweet only goes to that person, so the rest of your followers will not see that tweet. Now this is on the Twitter site. If your followers are using HootSuite or some other tools to read their tweets, then they will see you're "@" tweets. For the most part though, people do not use HootSuite or some other tool, so they will not see your "@" tweets.

So if you want to mention somebody in a tweet, such as, "Hi @kip_Piper. I saw your article at...", that tweet will go directly to that person.

Hashtags

A lot of people will use hashtags "#" to start or contribute to a conversation on a particular topic, as you can see in the screenshot below.

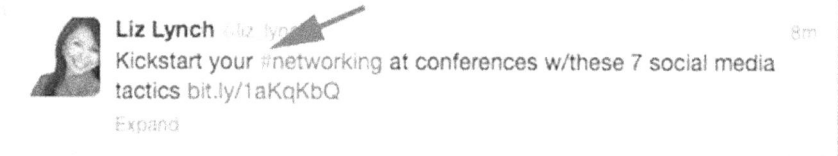

Liz Lynch Liz Lynch
Kickstart your #networking at conferences w/these 7 social media tactics bit.ly/1aKqKbQ
Expand

You can also use hashtags "#" to follow a topic that is trending worldwide or in a specific location. You can see these trends by clicking on the "#Discover" button at the top of your Twitter screen, as shown in the top red arrow in the screenshot below. Then look further down the left side of your Twitter page for a list of the current trending topics, as shown by the bottom red arrow in the screenshot below.

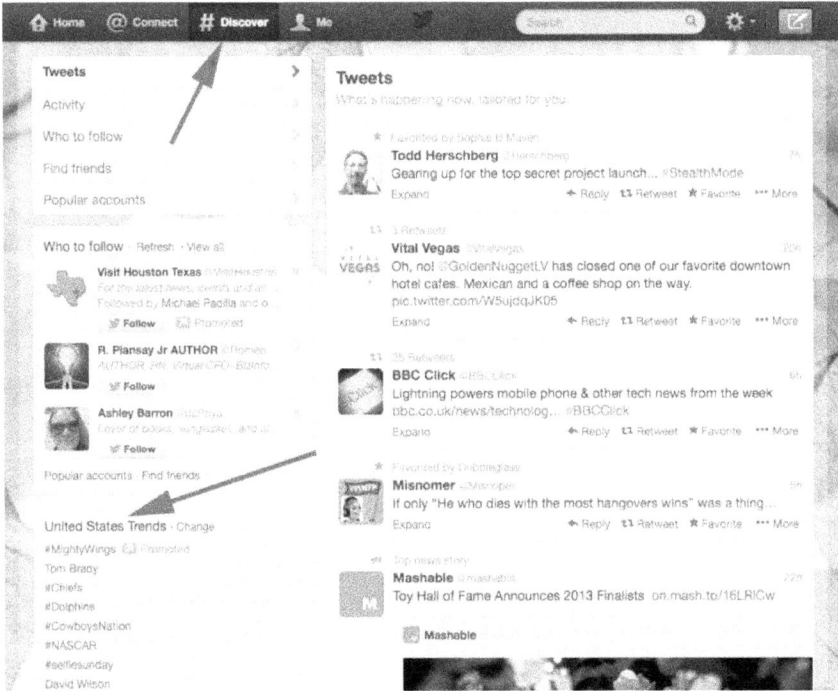

How are these hashtag "#" topics created? Typically it's a group of people who are following a particular conversation, so they put a hashtag "#" with a word or phrase identifying the topic. Then other people on Twitter can search that topic to see what people are talking about on that particular subject.

Replying

If you wish to reply to someone, simply hover your mouse over their message and a green menu bar will appear, as seen in the screenshot below. A reply box will open up, as also seen in the screenshot below, preaddressed to them and you simply type your message in the box and hit "Tweet" to send it to them.

Retweeting

You can also "retweet" someone's post. If you find someone has posted good content, and you want to share it with your audience and give credit to the person who posted it originally (which is proper Twitter etiquette), you would click on "Retweet", as shown in the screenshot below, and that will post their message to all of your followers and giving them credit.

Other items

When you click on the "@Connect" tab at the top of your Twitter screen, you will see where you can click on "Interactions" and "Mentions".

"Interactions" show not only when others have addressed specific tweets to you, but also when people have retweeted your posts or have begun following you, as seen in the screenshot below.

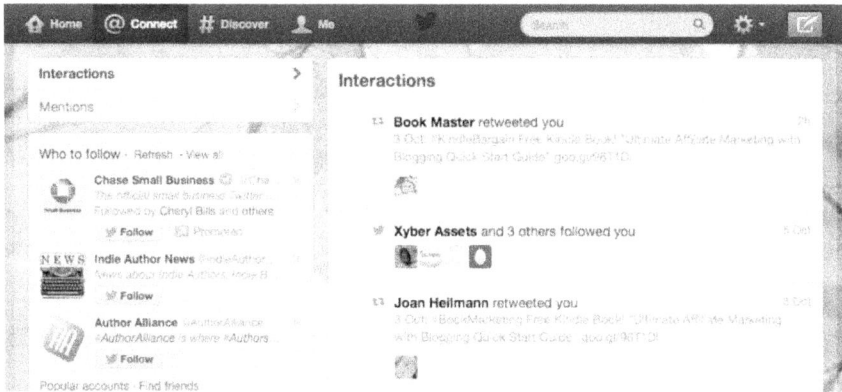

"Mentions" are a combination of retweets and direct messages using the "@" symbol and posts where others on Twitter have mentioned you in one of their posts, as you can see in the screenshot below.

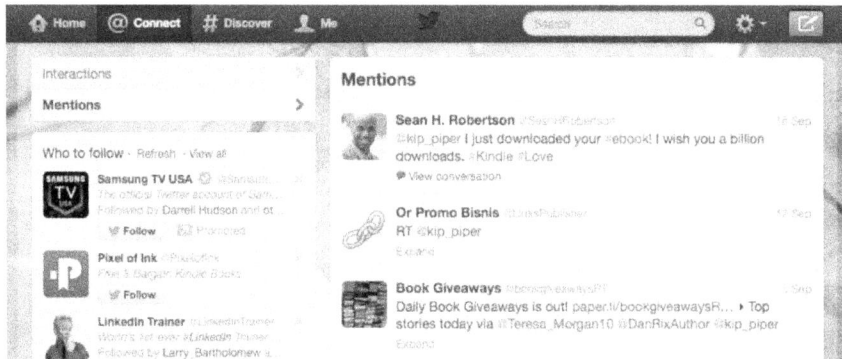

There are other things you can do with your Twitter account on the Twitter site, but Twitter site itself is not the best way to manage your Twitter time. Later on in this book I will introduce tools that would make your time and use of Twitter much more effective, more powerful, and more efficient.

Twitter can get pretty addictive. As it grows, it becomes a lot more fun and a lot more engaging, so you have to be careful with your time management. Later I will talk about using HootSuite, which is my favorite tool to manage your time. Even with HootSuite, it's good to have some kind of schedule or routine where you regularly and consistently communicate with your followers. As an example, you might get on Twitter in the morning, in the afternoon or in the evening. You could also use your mobile phone to communicate when you're, say, waiting at the doctor's office or when you're at lunch waiting for your food, etc. But ***don't*** spend all day on Twitter! It is very addictive! Make it a habit to only get on at the times that work best for you and spent only 5 to 10 minutes spurts here and there. You should be able to communicate effectively with your entire audience and do a good job with scheduled small amounts of time throughout the day. I have seen people experience great results using Twitter only for a few minutes a day. The tools I will share with you later in this book will make it really easy to get all the benefits out of Twitter without having to spend the entire day on it.

OPTIMIZING YOUR PROFILE FOR SUCCESS

This chapter is going to cover the important information you need to know about optimizing your profile for success. This information will help you set up your profile right from the beginning or you can edit your current profile so you get the best results.

Will first take a look at your "Settings". When you click on the drop-down arrow next to the "gear" symbol, you will see a menu with "Settings" towards the bottom, as shown in the screenshot below.

In the "Settings" screen, you will see where you can list a variety of information which you can customize.

I'm going to jump down to "Profile" first because there are important settings here that you need to be aware of. So please refer to the screenshot below.

Under "Name", sometimes when people sign up for Twitter, they make the mistake of putting in their name with no spaces, thinking that's going to be their username. This is actually your name as you wish it didn't appear on Twitter, so make sure you do separate the different parts of your name with spaces.

If you have already set up your Twitter profile and did not separate your name was spaces, you can edit your profile now and ad the spaces.

Why is it important to have your name separated? Because when people go to search for you, they're going to type in your name with spaces. If you don't have spaces in your name on your profile, then they cannot find you.

Also in your profile is where you set your profile picture. It is an image that you upload from your computer. It is also an image that you can change, if necessary.

In "Location", I put "Alpine, TX Texas" because some people search state names by their abbreviations, what other search state names spelled out.

The "Website" field is very important! When you look at a profile on Twitter, you have the ability to only see 17 characters of the person's website URL. The shorter your domain name the better. Most people don't realize this but most people have this set up to include the "www". Twitter used to include these characters in the website address seen on your profile. Now Twitter drops them, but I still like to omit them myself to keep things clean. However, test it yourself so you can see how your domain name appears in your profile. The majority of the domains out there work just fine. And even if your domain is longer than the 17 characters, it will still be hyperlinked to your website.

However, it's important to remember the theory that the more you can see someone's domain, the more likely a visitor is to click on it. Extensive testing has been done on this, and click-throughs tend to increase dramatically when the entire domain is visible on your profile.

Next is your "Bio", which is also very important! In your bio, be sure to use good keywords. As you can see in my profile below, I have also included that I'm a world traveler. Including personal items about yourself also helps start the relationship with your followers and build their trust. Remember, Twitter is a social network, so feel free to be a little social in your bio.

Your bio is really short – only 160 characters. Be brief, use good keywords, antisocial. This will help you get good results because people will be able to relate to you.

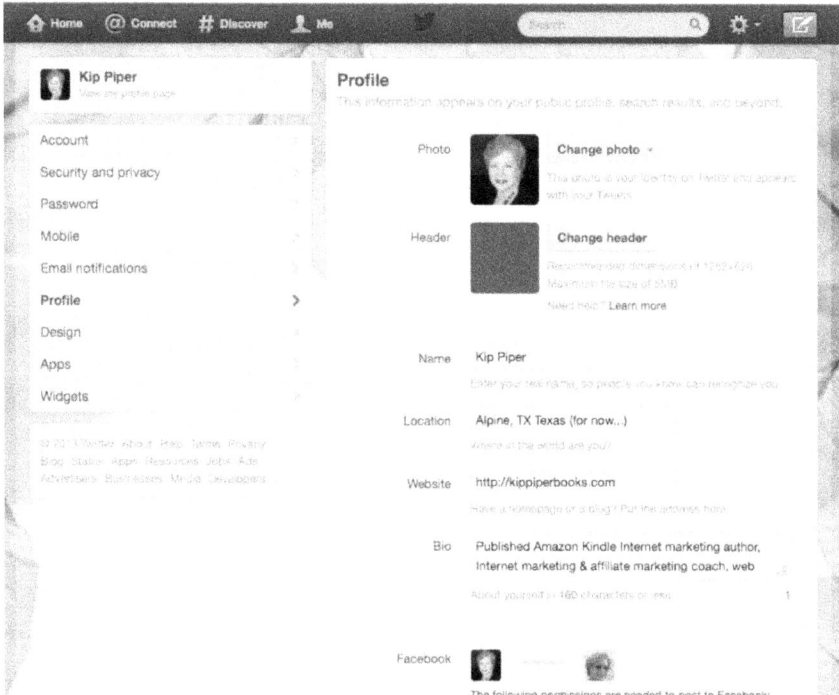

Never going to move up to your "Account" settings, as shown in the screenshot below.

For the "Username" field, if it's your personal Twitter account, I always suggest using your real username. This just makes it easier for people to identify who you are and earn their trust. If you use some strange name, like "greengrasspossum42", the trust factor will not resonate as well with people.

If you want to use your Twitter account for business, I suggest you set up a personal account and also a business account. Then in the "Bio" for your business account, I suggest that you mention that the account is handled by you, and include the Twitter username of your personal account, so they know a real person is handling it.

In the "Email" field, add the email address by which people know you best, because this means they can also search for you on Twitter by using your email address.

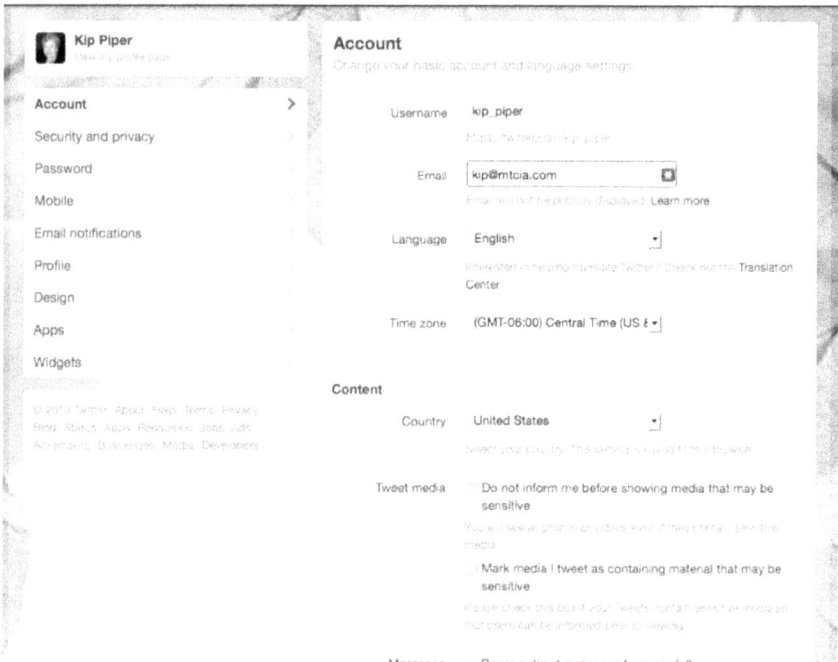

Next is "Email Notifications". As you can see in the screenshot below, you want to disable all of these notifications. If you want to check to receive the Twitter newsletter, that's your choice. But you definitely do not want to be bombarded with email and/or text notifications when you have new followers, when you receive direct messages, etc. I had a colleague who received over 1000 emails per night for a few nights when he posted something that generated a bunch of new followers. It was a nightmare! The tools that we will discuss later in this book will help you monitor everything that you need without being bombarded by the stuff you don't.

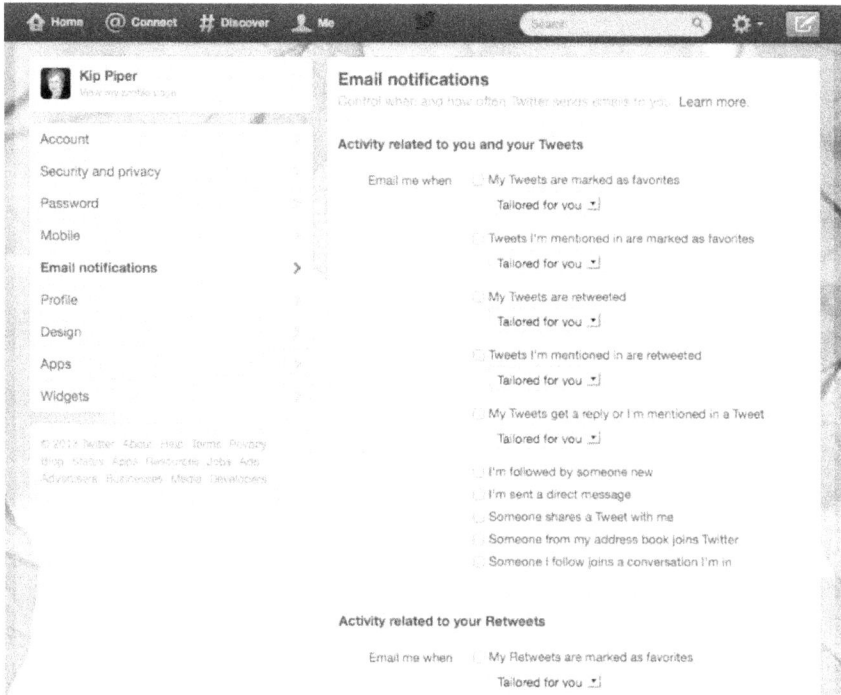

Next is "Design". This is your background artwork for your Twitter profile. You can either pick a premade seem, as shown in the examples below, or upload your own background artwork. I really don't think it makes that big of a difference. You cannot make any of the background clickable. Depending on your goals of how you want to use your Twitter account, you might want to make the background image more marketable. Later on in this book I will give you websites where you can have custom background images created.

One thing in your design that is important is the color of your links. I highly recommend that you keep the color of your links the default blue. There have been extensive tests done that, if the color is changed, people are less likely to click on them.

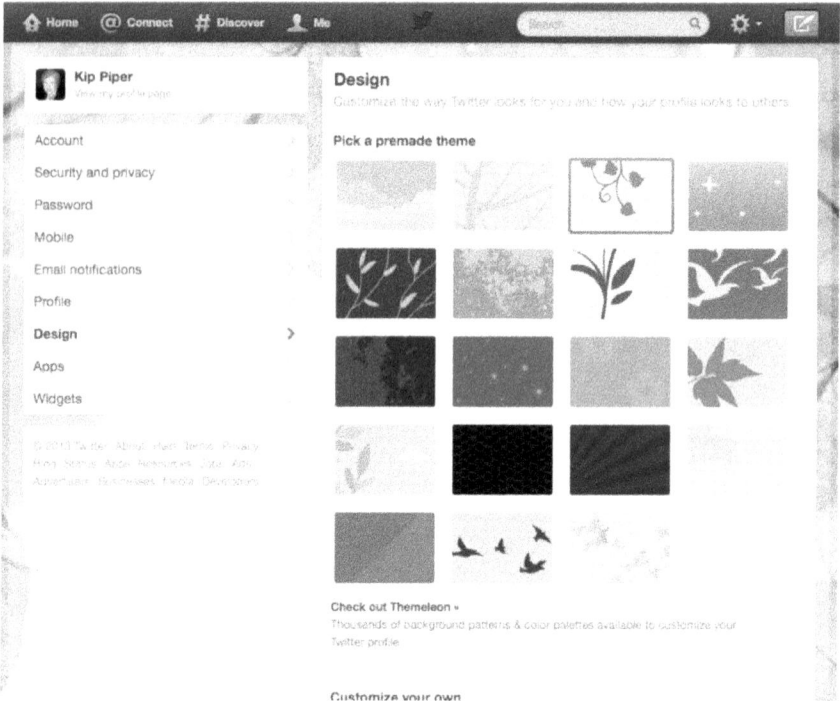

Last is your "Apps". There are a lot of third-party applications that you might use such as Facebook or LinkedIn or HootSuite, that require your permission to connect to your Twitter account. As you can see in the screenshot below, you will see a list of applications for which you have granted access to your Twitter account. It's a good idea to go through this list every once in a while and delete the ones that you're not using anymore. You do that simply by clicking on the "Revoke Access" button. We will talk later about some specific third-party applications that you should use.

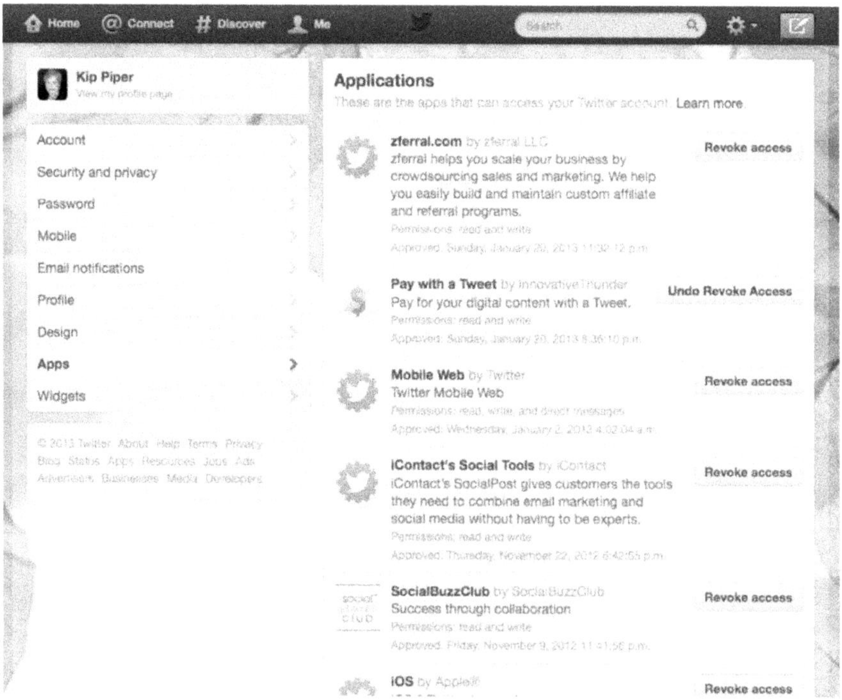
Home
Connect
Discover
Me
Kip Piper
Account
Security and privacy
Password
Mobile
Email notifications
Profile
Design
Apps
Widgets
Applications
Learn more
zferral.com
zferral helps you scale your business by crowdsourcing sales and marketing. We help you easily build and maintain custom affiliate and referral programs.
Revoke access
Pay with a Tweet
Pay for your digital content with a Tweet.
Undo Revoke Access
Mobile Web
Twitter Mobile Web
Revoke access
iContact's Social Tools
iContact's SocialPost gives customers the tools they need to combine email marketing and social media without having to be experts.
Revoke access
SocialBuzzClub
Success through collaboration
Revoke access
iOS
Revoke access

WHAT YOU SHOULD BE SAYING
FOR SUCCESS ON TWITTER

We talked about this briefly in the earlier part of this book, but I really want to get deeply into this in this section. In the following chapters, we will cover:

- How to write tweaks that engage
- How long tweets should be and what they should say
- Went to say what – optimal times of day
- Content – ideas of what to tweet

WRITING TWEETS TO ENGAGE

There are a few "Golden Rules" to keep in mind.

The first one to consider is the length of your tweet. Twitter allows for 140 characters per tweet.

If you want to put out a tweet, your goal most of the time should be to put out quality content that will be retweeted, such as a link to an article or a quote, etc. You always want to keep your character count under 120 characters. This allows someone to retweet your post and have enough space to add your "@name" to give you credit for your original post. If you put out a tweet that is 140 characters long, people would have to edit or cut it down in order to retweet and maintain the essence of the original post and also give you credit for the post. You need to keep it simple and easy for others to retweet your posts.

There is Power in Retweeting

When someone retweets your content, it's pretty impressive! When someone retweets you or speaks back to you, everyone who follows them can potentially see their post.

As an example, Writer.ly retweeted about one of my books. As you can see the screenshot below, when I looked at a thumbnail of their profile, they have over 35,000 followers. This means that my original tweet has now potentially reached an additional 35,000 people!

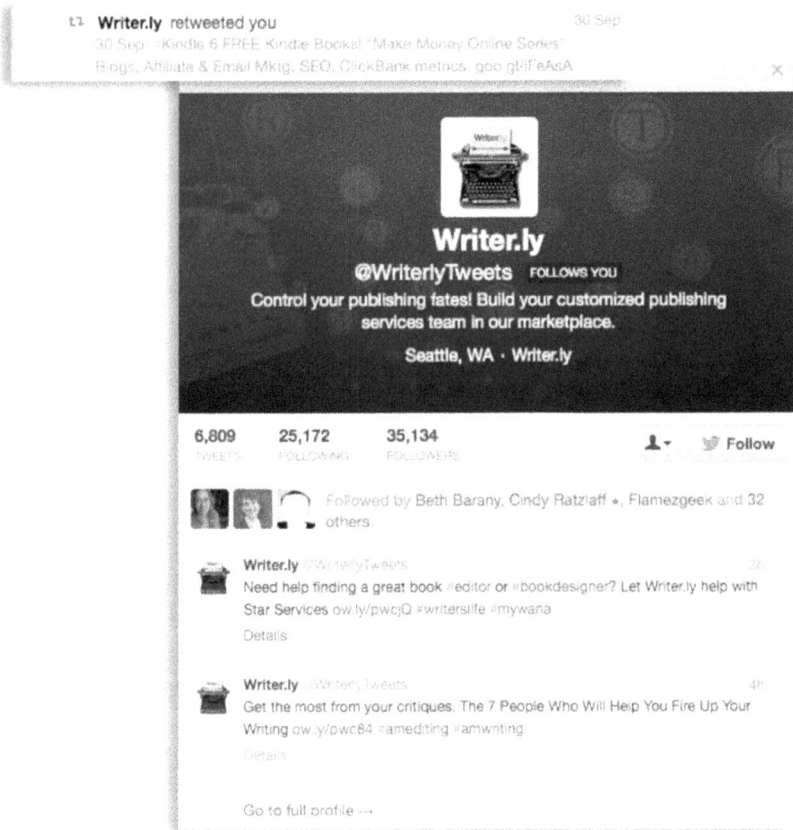

In addition, because their followers have seen my original tweet, the number of followers that I have almost immediately increases dramatically. That is the power of retweeting.

By putting out information and having it retweeted, it drives even more traffic back to your page, which in turn adds subscribers to your email list.

Writing Tweets to Engage

Your goals should always be to get retweeted and to engage with your audience. There are a variety of ways that you can accomplish this.

You can ask questions of your followers. For instance:

- Ask them if you should have steak or sushi?
- Ask them what kind of music should you listen to?

- What business book should you read?
- If you need help with your business, ask questions related to that.

When you ask questions, be sure to watch for responses over the following few minutes. You can reply back and start conversations with those who posted, especially those that are new followers, and develop relationships with them.

Here are some more ideas of content:

Quotes always go over really well. In fact, quotes always seem to get the highest number of retweets. Remember, quotes go better in the morning. You can use sites like Digg or Reddit that aggregate content to find good quotes. Google is also great place to search for and find quotes.

News headlines – especially for your niche – can be very effective. With Google, you can search down through their News feed and get quotes from within the last week, last day, and even breaking news within the last hour. You could be the first person to tweet out a story to your followers, which can be pretty significant in establishing authority, generating retweets, and increasing your followers.

Cool Strategies to Drive Traffic

If you have or can find a great photo that is just dying for a caption, hold a Caption Contest on your Twitter feed. Offer a $20 Amazon gift card for the best caption. Yes, it will cost you $20, but it'll be the best $20 you spend because it will drive traffic and build your brand.

Another strategy is to hold a poll on your website. You post on your Twitter account that you're conducting a poll and the link to your website within your Twitter post. As variation on the Caption Contest, you can have four possible captions on your poll and have your followers vote for the best caption. Again, offer an Amazon gift card to the winner.

HOW TO AVOID GETTING BANNED

Twitter has several rules that you need to pay attention to – really important ones.

We talked earlier about growing your Twitter following. The most important thing you should ***not*** do – to keep yourself from getting banned – is simply don't "unfollow" people too soon. A lot of people make the mistake of following a bunch of people and then unfollowing them before 24 hours have passed. When people unfollow others within 10, 12, 18 hours after following them, this throws up a huge red flag in the eyes of Twitter. The best advice I can give you is pay attention to this. **Do not unfollow people.** If you use a software, or one of the websites which I will discuss later in this book in the Tools chapter, to unfollow people, wait until at least 24 hours has passed.

Now if you unfollow one or two people right after you follow them, that's no big deal. It's when you unfollow in masses that it becomes a problem. This is the most obvious thing that's always going to get you banned.

Another thing that will get you banned is putting out information that is just a nonstop spew of sales messages or tweets that are asking people to take an action to go buy something or anything that could be viewed as spamming. So keep that in mind and be conscious of that.

The bottom line is, if you provide value and you're someone who is an asset to the community, you're not going to have any issues. How does Twitter know if you're an asset to the community? Well, it's simple. It's your username.

How many times is your username mentioned in a tweet?
Are people talking to you?
Are they retweeting your stuff?

Are they interacting with you?

Are you interacting back?

That's what Twitter wants: the more interactive the better for them and the network.

So be that kind of tweeter. Don't get on there and just send out a tweet here or there, or send out messages that are spamming or selling a lot of stuff. That will get you in trouble.

Here is another key thing to do. Before you ramp up the growth on your account, make sure you have send out at least 10 to 20 tweets. If not, it's another big red flag for Twitter. Occasionally you might see accounts with no tweets and 4,000 or 5,000 followers. That can be an issue as well. These are *not* the accounts to emulate! While they may fly under the radar for awhile, they always end up getting banned. So make sure you have several tweets before you grow your audience.

Another thing to consider is the use of automated direct messages and the potential of getting blocked.

First we'll talk about getting blocked. If someone blocks you or reports you for spamming, that will be a bad mark against you in the eyes of Twitter.

Another thing is direct messages. I've never had a problem nor had my account banned because of automated direct messages. I think it's because I provide value, interact with people, and I try to do a good job on Twitter.

If you're using direct messages, make sure you change your automated direct minute messages from time to time so they don't say the same things all of the time. If you're using a service like Social Oomph or software, also make sure you change the links along with the messages that go out. We'll talk in the Tools chapter about some tools that can show you how good of a job you were doing or how Twitter views you, your actions, and the quality of your content.

It's important to remember that, if you're **not** using Twitter a lot, don't use automated direct messages because it will get you in trouble with Twitter. But if you are using Twitter a lot, interacting with people, and engaging, then you should be fine using automated direct messages.

Another red flag is setting up multiple accounts from the same IP address (from the same computer). If you want to set up multiple accounts and fly under Twitter's radar, you will want to use different IP addresses. If you don't know how to do this, there are services on the Internet that will help you with this.

Another red flag that you're setting up multiple accounts is using the same email address for all of the accounts. Make sure you use a different email address for each Twitter account.

If you ever do have a problem with Twitter, the good news is that Twitter keeps the lines of communication open through their support. If your account gets banned or you lose your account, you can always contact for the support and get it set back up.

TOOLS FOR TWITTER

In this final section of the book, I want to go over some tools that will really help you maximize your time on Twitter. I will share with you some of the tools that I use that really make a big difference, plus a few others to consider. We will also cover some secrets on how to drive a lot of traffic using Twitter.

NOTE: All recommended tools and links to their websites is also found in the **Resources** section at the end of this book.

HOOTSUITE

HootSuite http://kippiperbooks.com/hootsuite is an amazing tool to save yourself a lot of time. It does everything that Twitter does, but with a more efficient layout. As you can see the screenshot below, the HootSuite panel can be set up to show a variety of feeds from your Twitter account. In my account, shown below, you can see my "Sent Tweets", "Mentions", "Retweets", and "Scheduled Tweets". This is how I set up my Twitter panel. You can set it up to see other things from your Twitter account, such as "Direct Messages", specific lists, and more.

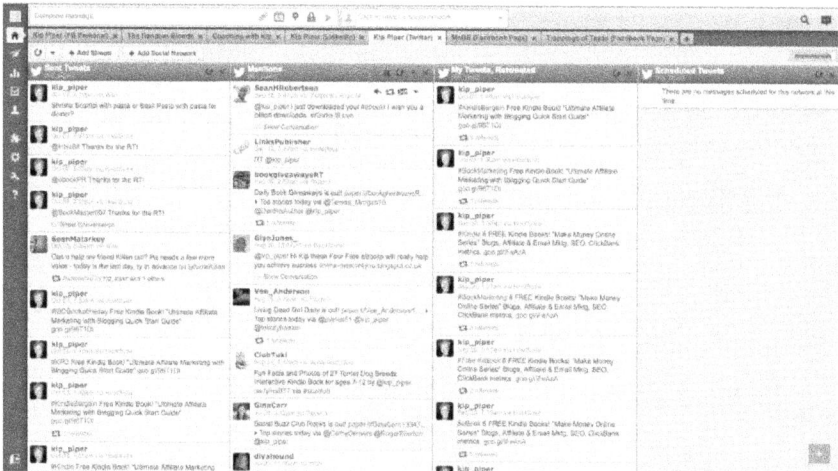

Another thing I like about HootSuite is that you can connect to all of your different social media accounts, such as other Twitter accounts, your Facebook personal profile and Facebook pages, and LinkedIn profile.

HootSuite also works if you have multiple Twitter accounts, which we discussed earlier on how to properly set up.

There are a variety of advantages to having all of your networks in one place.

For instance, you can send one message and have it simultaneously broadcast to all of your profiles and pages. Or you can have one message go to only a few select profiles or pages. HootSuite is a huge timesaver in this regard.

Another neat thing is "Drafts". Here you can save your most common messages that you put out. I often invite people from Twitter to connect with me on Facebook, which is a great way to build your list on Facebook. People spent time on Twitter and they spent time on Facebook, so this way you can get them in both places.

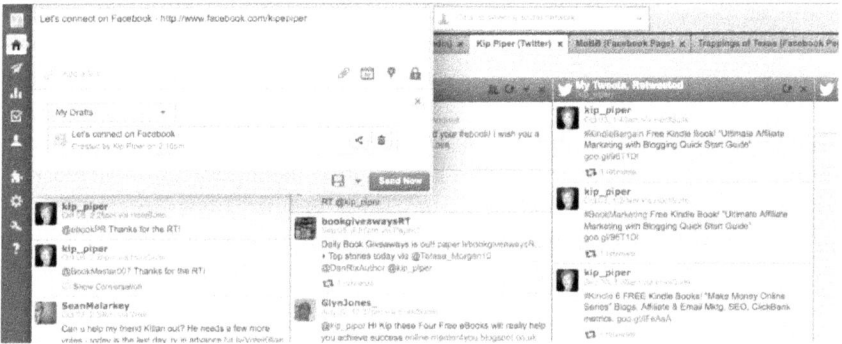

A real valuable feature is being able to schedule messages. You simply write your message and the message field, as shown below, and then set a day, time and network or networks were you wanted broadcast. This is a great tool to save time and effort on your part.

If you notice in the screenshot above, there is a small field called "Add a link…". This is a great URL shortening tool. How you use it is to type in the full URL that you want to include in your message. Then a "Shrink" button appears. Simply click on the "Shrink" button and HootSuite will automatically shorten your URL and add it to the end of your message. This is very valuable since you are limited by the number of characters you can use in your messages, especially Twitter which is limited to 140 characters. By being able to shorten your URL, you're not using valuable real estate in your message for just your URL.

If you want to be able to track for Google analytics where your clicks are coming from, you can click on the "gear" icon to the right of where you type in your URL and it opens an "Advanced" settings window, as you can see in the screenshot below. You then simply choose "Google Analytics" from the "Add custom URL parameters" drop down. You then customize each parameter, such as I have done by adding "twitter" as the value to the first parameter. You can also add the "medium" and a "campaign" name. These can be whatever you wanted them to be. What happens is that HootSuite adds code to the ULR that's going to be shrunk and then transmits this data to Google analytics when people click on the link.

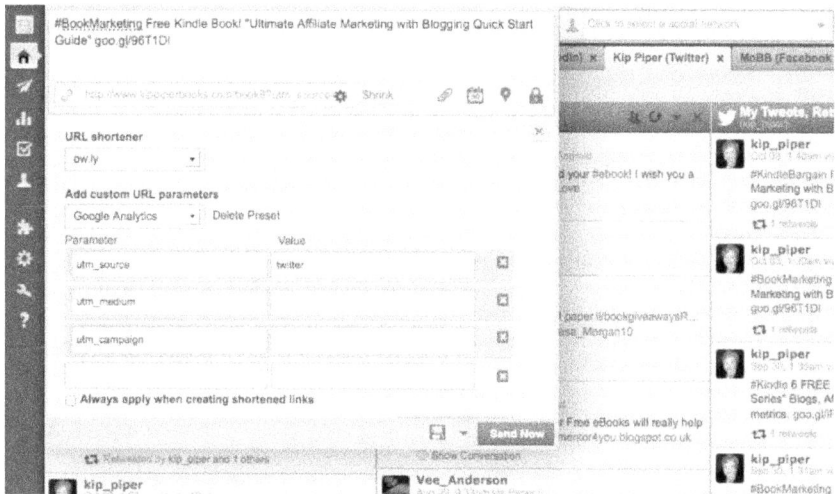

A lot of times when people click links through a mobile phone, they're not trackable as to where they're coming from. But by using this feature, it's can't exactly track from where your links are coming.

So you can change it to say Facebook, or LinkedIn, as well as Twitter. And then post them separately to your streams within your HootSuite account. By tracking them by stream, you can see where the most clicks are coming from. This is a great way to test the traffic and understand what are your traffic sources.

If you click on the s\Stats icon in the left-hand menu, as shown in the screenshot below, you have access to a variety of reports that show the activity on your various streams. If you use the HootSuite URL shortener, you can track your stats of click throughs.

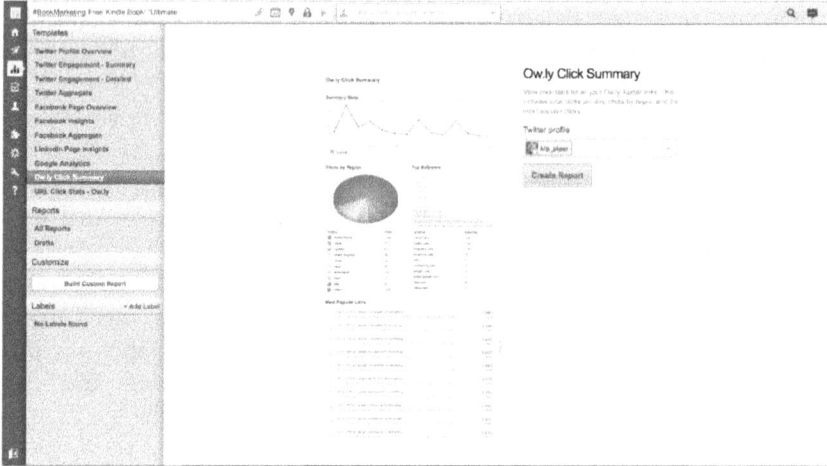

Below is the report if you want to look at your Google Analytics. You can change the profile from the drop-down to choose to see your Twitter stats, your Facebook stats, your LinkedIn stats, etc.

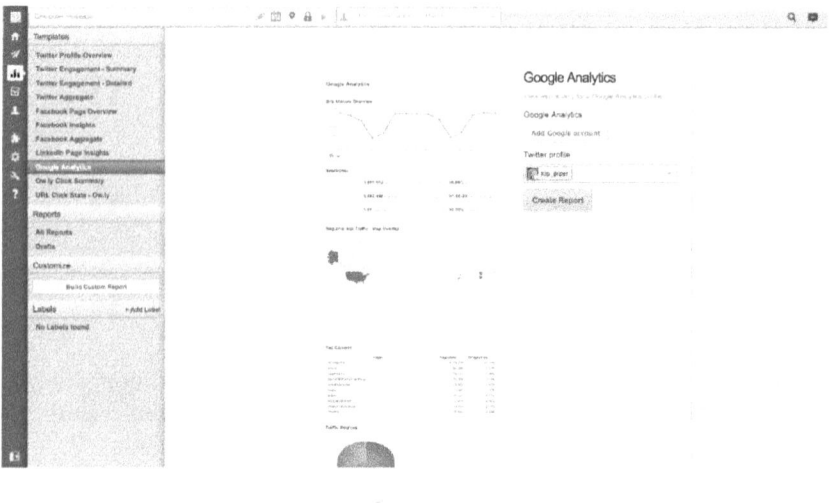

Be sure to go through the HootSuite tutorials and search for YouTube video tutorials to make sure you get the most out of your **HootSuite http://kippiperbooks.com/hootsuite** service and all of its cool services.

OTHER TOOLS

TweetDeck

A lot of people use **TweetDeck http://tweetdeck.com/**. TweetDeck is software that you download to your computer. (I personally prefer HootSuite because it's web-based, which means I can log into my account from anywhere to check and manage my account.)

TweetDeck does a few things that HootSuite doesn't. I've used both HootSuite and TweetDeck, and I really prefer **HootSuite** **http://kippiperbooks.com/hootsuite**. However TweetDeck is good if you don't like HootSuite.

Topsy

Topsy http://topsy.com is a great tool to search and discover some cool information about your tweeting. You can search for your username to do a variety reports, as you can see the screenshot below. If your name is similar to others, be sure to search for your username with the "@" symbol, like I did - @kip_piper. Then your results are likely to be more accurate.

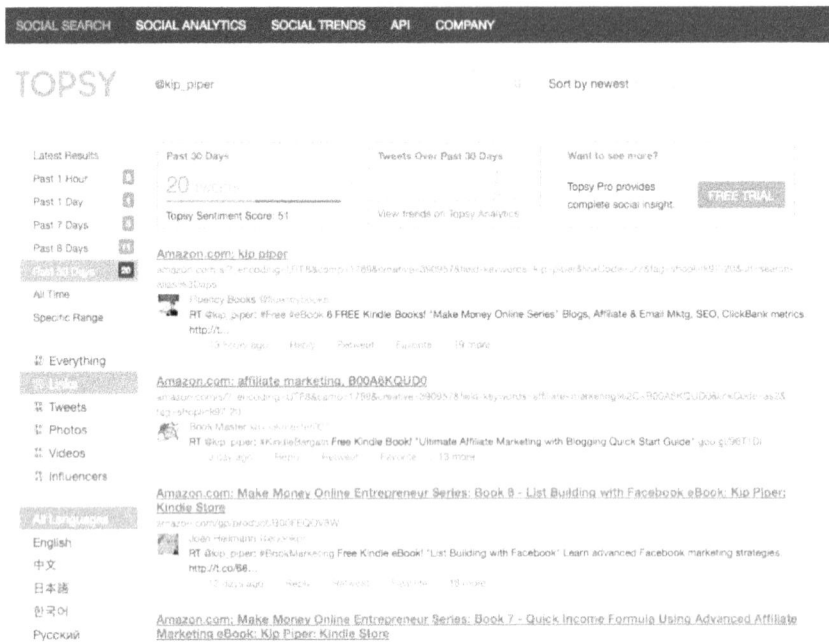

If you look through the Topsy interface, you will see different reports. You can look at your most popular posts, you can sort by photos, links, videos, etc. It's a good tool to discover what types of tweets are working, or people are actually liking and retweeting, and what types of tweets are not working.

Klout

Klout http://klout.com/home measures your influence on Twitter and Facebook. This is a great tool to measure your influence. The score in general indicates how good of a job you're doing. People that have higher Klout scores generally are more active Twitter users.

As you can see from the screenshot below, my score as of this writing is 52. When I am more active on Twitter and I have my tweets retweeted, my score has been as high as in the 70s.

Twitter Counter

Twitter Counter http://twittercounter.com/ is a tool to measure your growth on Twitter. As you can see from the screenshot below, it gives you a graph of your growth over time.

One thing that is interesting is that you can look at your growth based on your tweets. This will give you an idea of what types of tweets are more popular.

Bit.ly

Bit.ly http://www.Bit.ly is a great URL shortener that can help you track your traffic on Twitter. You would use this instead of the built-in HootSuite URL shortener. By using the Bit.ly, your Elshor in her, you can get all of your Twitter stats consolidated on the Bit.ly website. What a cool feature is that it offers your stats in real time. So when you send out a tweet, you can immediately see how it is doing. It has a lot of other great features, including tracking your retweets and an automatic URL shortener tool for your browser.

A great reporting feature, as seen in the screenshot below, is a summary of all of your clicks over the last 30 days.

Your Bit.ly Metrics Summary

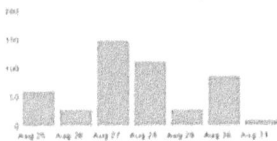

467 Clicks on Your Bit.ly Links

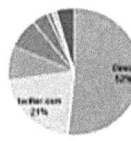

20 Referring Domains
From 36 Total Pages

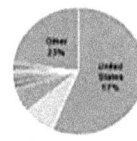

32 Countries

Referrers Detail	
Referring Site	Click(s)
Email Clients (M AIR Apps and Direct) »	241
twitter.com »	99
Registered Applications »	42
hootsuite.com »	36
www.facebook.com »	18

Locations Detail	
Country	Click(s)
United States	264
Other	68
Canada	36
United Kingdom	29
France	8

In the next section I will be going over tips to drive traffic. Of the things in this section, it's important to be influential, to do a good job with your tweets, and provide value. This is what will ultimately drive traffic.

Social Oomph

Social Oomph http://www.kippiperbooks.com/socialoomph gives you the ability to send a direct message, schedule tweets, etc., as you can see from the screenshot below. So if you're not using another tool, such as HootSuite, you can use Social Oomph to carry out these functions.

SOCIAL OMPH

Schedule updates for your Facebook account, Facebook Page, and Facebook Group. Click Social Accounts, Add New Account in the menu.

Kip Piper
Free
4:53 PM

Main Landing Page
Schedule New Update
Schedule New Photo
Schedule Blog Post
Shorten URL
Social Accounts
Scheduled Updates
Direct Messages
Followers/Friends
Blogs
Statistics
Monitors
My User Account
Help
About Us

Hi Kip. Customize your home menu by hiding the sections you don't need to see.

Click Here to Test Drive
SocialOomph Professional

Frequently Used Features [hide]
- Add a New Scheduled Status Update
- View All My Status Updates
- Vet My New Followers
- Manage My Social Accounts (Edit, Delete)
- View Graphs of My Twitter Statistics
- Submit a Support Ticket

Social Accounts [hide]
- Add a New Twitter Account
- Test My Blog for Compatibility
- Manage My Social Accounts (Edit, Delete)
- Create My Extended Twitter Profile
- View My Automation Status & Statistics
- View Graphs of My Twitter Statistics

Friends & Followers [hide]
- Vet My New Followers

Monitors [hide]
- View The Predefined System Channels
- View My @Mentions and/or Retweets
- Manage My Tweet Keyword Tracking & Alerts

Direct Messages [hide]
- Purge My Twitter DM Inbox

My Account [hide]
- Start My Free Professional Trial
- Upgrade My Account To Professional

DRIVING TRAFFIC WITH TWITTER

Here are the basic tips to drive traffic with Twitter:

The basic rule for driving traffic is to tweet content from your website. In other words, if you just wrote a blog and posted it on your website, then tweet to your followers the title of the blog, a quick call to action, and a link to the blog.

Most of the successful influencers on Twitter tweet content four times a day. Remember, not all of your followers are on Twitter at the same time. For instance, you could tweet the same tweet in the morning, in the afternoon, in the early evening, and either late evening or overnight.

If you are worried about someone getting upset because you are retweeting content over and over, change your subject line. In other words, if you're tweeting a blog post and you're using the title of the blog post in your first set of tweets, change that blog title to something else that conveys the same meaning and information.

It's not a good idea to send the same content out over and over without putting different tweets in between. However if you do, you can delete your earlier tweets of the same content from your Twitter feed.

Remember, you can use **HootSuite** **http://kippiperbooks.com/hootsuite** to schedule all of these tweets.

Retweet Influential People

Follow on Twitter the influential people in your niche. Create a list in Twitter (or HootSuite or other tool you may be using) of these people and others with whom you want to connect. Then regularly retweet their posts to your followers. Occasionally they will retweet you back! I have had that happen to me. It's not only a great compliment to you, but it also drives traffic to your site.

Retweet, interact and engage with the powerful, influential people in your industry, become friends with them, and you'll be surprised how they will just naturally help drive traffic to your site.

You can even, once a month or so, ask the top 10 or so to retweet one of your posts for you. Make sure you do not abuse this privilege, only do it once in a while, and make sure you are asking them to retweet exceptional, quality content. But you'll be amazed that most of them will retweet something for you.

SUMMARY OF TWITTER

Now that you've completed this book, here is what's important to remember about Twitter.

While you need to understand the general concepts, Twitter is all about engaging a large free audience that you can then convert to your email list. When we are talking about Twitter, remember that you won't have people attention for a long period of time. Twitter is like ADHD on steroids! It's these little, quick messages. So when you're thinking about headlines and the type of content you're using on Twitter, be engaging, be quick, share links, get people to either:

- Opt in to your list
- Go to your squeeze page
- Register for free webinar
- Read your blog post with an opt in

Twitter is not a great place to sell, but it's a great place to build a presence.

One thing that is awesome is that a lot of people on Twitter are engaging with photographs. We have talked about quotes, blog posts, and other types of content. But photographs are also a great way to engage people on Twitter. Photographs also help your followers get to know you a little bit better in your personal and business life.

Always, always, always remember this about Twitter:

- You want to respect your followers.
- You want to be consistent with the content that you deliver and the way you communicate to them.

- And always think about ways you can move your followers to your email list where you can market your products and services or affiliate products and services more aggressively via email rather than directly on Twitter.

BONUS MATERIALS

Below is the link to this book's bonus material. I have developed this tools from my own experience as well as compiled from tools I have used from various training courses I have taken.

The mind map is built in XMind software. You can download a free version of XMind from http://www.xmind.net.

The item is also available as a PDF.

Strategic_Plan_List_Building_with_Twitter.xmind
http://www.kippiperbooks.com/make-money-online/book09/Strategic_Plan_List_Building_with_Twitter.xmind

Strategic_Plan_List_Building_with_Twitter.pdf
http://www.kippiperbooks.com/make-money-online/book09/Strategic_Plan_List_Building_with_Twitter.pdf

RESOURCES

HootSuite
http://kippiperbooks.com/hootsuite

The best tool I have found for managing all of your social network profiles in one place from anywhere.

TweetDeck
http://tweetdeck.com/

A software program that you download to your computer to manage your social network profiles.

Topsy
http://topsy.com

A search tool that reveals interesting data about results from your tweeting.

Klout
http://klout.com/home

Measures your influence on Twitter and Facebook

Twitter Counter
http://twittercounter.com/

Measures your growth on Twitter

Bit.ly
http://www.Bit.ly

Great URL shortener with real time statistics and other great features.

Social Oomph
http://www.kippiperbooks.com/socialoomph

Similar but not as powerful as HootSuite

MORE KINDLE BOOKS BY KIP PIPER

Ultimate Affiliate Marketing with Blogging Quick Start Guide
http://www.kippiperbooks.com/UltimateGuide

Make Money Online Entrepreneur Series:

Below are just a few of the books in this series. To browse the entire series, go to:
http://www.kippiperbooks.com/makemoneyonlineseries

Book 1 – Freeing Up Your Time – VA's, Outsourcing & Goal Setting
http://www.kippiperbooks.com/book1

Book 2 – Your Core Business, Niche & Competitors
http://www.kippiperbooks.com/book2

Book 3 – Blogs & Emails: Your Link with Your Customers
http://www.kippiperbooks.com/book3

Book 4 – Affiliate Marketing 101
http://www.kippiperbooks.com/book4

Book 5 - Driving Traffic with Organic SEO
http://www.kippiperbooks.com/book5

Book 6 – Power of Email Marketing
http://www.kippiperbooks.com/book6

Book 7 – Quick Income Formula with Advanced Affiliate Marketing
http://www.kippiperbooks.com/book7

Book 8 – List Building with Facebook
http://www.kippiperbooks.com/book8

Book 9 – List Building with Twitter
http://www.kippiperbooks.com/book9

Book 10 - List Building with LinkedIn
http://www.kippiperbooks.com/book10

ONE LAST THING…

As you can probably tell from my writing, my intention is to inspire and support more people to build a better financial future. It's a tough economy today, and I think personal growth in the field of small business is more important than ever before. Even though I have well over 20 years of experience as a successful small business owner and online entrepreneur, I don't have all the answers. In fact I'm still learning myself, I just have my own opinions, experiences and a passion for being my own boss to guide me through life.

Thank you purchasing my eBook and for taking the time to read it. I hope you enjoyed it and found value within its pages.

If you did I would really appreciate your support by taking the time to write a review for me on Amazon. Reviews really help the authors you enjoy to get noticed in a crowded marketplace, and it would allow me to continue writing the books for this series and other business books.

Please visit the URL below to let me know your thoughts:

http://kippiperbooks.com/book9

All of my books are offered completely FREE on the launch and I want to reward loyal readers by offering my new books to them FREE of charge when they are released.

So please visit my website KipPiperBooks.com and either download your free copy of "28-Day Small Business Profit Plan: The Quick Start Guide to Business Success" or just sign up to my newsletter in order to be kept informed when the next release is due. I hate spam, so I promise I won't share your information with anyone – not for love nor money!

Good luck! I wish you every success in your personal and business endeavors.

www.ingramcontent.com/pod-product-compliance
Lightning Source LLC
Chambersburg PA
CBHW070811210326
41520CB00011B/1907